LOVE IF WE CAN STAND IT

Poems by Bruce F. Kawin

THAMES RIVER PRESS

Love If We Can Stand It

THAMES RIVER PRESS
An imprint of Wimbledon Publishing Company Limited (WPC)
Another imprint of WPC is Anthem Press (www.anthempress.com)

First published in the United Kingdom in 2012 by

THAMES RIVER PRESS
75-76 Blackfriars Road
London SE1 8HA

www.thamesriverpress.com

A CIP record for this book is available from the British Library.

ISBN 978-0-85728-921-6

Cover design by Laura Carless.

This title is also available as an eBook.

CONTENTS

Earlier versions of some of these poems (and a few unrevised ones) appeared in limited editions from Angelfish Press and in *Chronicle, Confrontation, Dreamworks, Epoch, The Green Horse for Poetry, Hanging Loose, The Paris Review, Rolling Stock, Student Filmmakers* and *Writers' Forum.*

A NEW SONG

song of the radio
song of the deer
song of the river
song of songs

1

I am a radio, night's hand on the dial.
Thanks to night I receive you, and what is in your heart
vibrates and pulses in me like a wave.

2

Deer are sacred. They never scavenge. Their proper food
uncurls its leaves in the full pride of the earth,
rising to meet them in every soil and weather.

One night the moon impelled me up this mountain.
I heard a shadow move in the bright grass.

3

God's humor is tough as the bones that stand inside us.
He has given us logic to understand the jokes.

God hung a veil between me and the river of rest.
It was bright with the sound of water, soft with wind.

It pulled me but stood in the way.
This morning we drew it aside.

I am the river.

4

They taught us never to say love in a love poem
and with the diligence of a lover I believed them.
In the ninth grade they posted Go Away Cliché
and in the rooms where poets gathered to learn their craft
they made it clear that love, the heart, and beauty,
although subjects for poetry, were not its terms.

After I had lived a hundred and fifty years
and had written many books
I found myself looking across a field of wheat.
My hand relaxed open in the wind
and moved through the buds as if across your cheek.
Now I can tell you about it.

CARDBOARD

1

When the overwhelming slams you
words go cardboard.

Shove them away
and the world

roars with feeling—
not silent but no symbols.

2

You try to fill the absence that is killing you
with stories, to say

she loved sex and her cats
he loved to play Bach and cook

but the gap reaches
out to no hand.

MENU

1

You meet on a lawn. A friend makes the introductions.
   You agree to meet later.

You meet in a catacomb.
   A skull tumbles
   from the reliquary bone-pile.

You meet in a restaurant with one table open.
   You decide to eat together.

You meet in a seminar. Everyone around you
   is missing the point, but you see it.
   You go out and talk for hours over coffee.

You meet on a camping trip.
   You have the only two zip-together bags
   of the same manufacture.

You meet like words in a short sentence.
   You have turned your attention to the other words before
   but now you see your error.

You meet in a bar. It's hard to hear.
   You have nothing to do that evening.

You meet in a deserted post office
   mailing love letters to others in the middle of the night.

You meet in a room whose walls defy dimension.

You meet at a party.
    You both flunked Dancing 1-A.

✦

You run into each other again after fifteen years
    in a deserted San Francisco movie house.
    Who else could be as interested as you
    in *The Wolf Man*, *Sherlock Jr.*, and *L'Age d'or*?

Everyone's talking about it
    so you get two seats for that downtown musical.

You go to a cattle roundup in midwinter.
    Around the fire for the branding irons
    your breath makes smoke.

Suddenly you are naked and everything's easy.

Somebody has a room she isn't using.
    You go there and talk about your other lovers.

You're over the edge in minutes.

The hotel costs forty in this neighborhood.
    The picture's an ocean oil stamped on cardboard.

It's impossible, but you're being touched
    everywhere at once, inside and out.
    The body is water, the muscles are birds flying over.
    You've never seen so much sweat.

✦

You both fade away with the walls,
    wake in separate rooms.

You wake in a Mayan ruin.
    The birds are loud.
    You swim in the river
    and peel the red bananas.

You switch on the *Today* show
    and pour the orange juice.
    You've each got appointments at nine.

You go out for breakfast at your favorite place.
    The daylight is ravenous for you to join it.

✦

The mysterious letter arrives.
    One of you leaves town,
    the other goes to sit in a park.

You hate each other
    every day
    more deeply and more truly.

You become indispensable
    like the hot in hot sauce.

You sleep with others
    but always want to come back.

Why wreck a good thing?
    The breakup is refreshingly bitter.

There is a revolution
    and both of you are freed.

✦

When the dog has her puppies
    your kids like to show them around
    holding them aloft in little hands.

You invest in a cabin
    and live there for seven years.

You are rescued by helicopter
    but ask them to drop you off
    in the Middle Ages.

The back yard is crazy with flowers.
    You lie down together.

2

You meet on a lawn. A friend makes the introductions.
You go to a cattle roundup in midwinter.
You wake in a Mayan ruin
and peel the red bananas.
You are rescued by helicopter
but ask them to drop you off in the Middle Ages.

You meet in a restaurant with one table open.
You decide to eat together.
You're over the edge in minutes.
The breakup is refreshingly bitter.

You meet in a room whose walls defy dimension.
Suddenly you are naked and everything's easy.
If it's all right, you'd like to change that:
you'll just have the puppies.

You meet in a seminar.
You run into each other again after fifteen years
in a deserted San Francisco movie house.
There is a revolution
and both of you are freed.
The back yard is crazy with flowers.
You lie down together.

You meet like words in a short sentence.
It's impossible, but you're being touched
everywhere at once, inside and out.
The body is water, the muscles are birds flying over.
You go out for breakfast at your favorite place.
The daylight is ravenous for you to join it.

OLD FRANKENSTEIN

The old man never calls.
He quit making us
settled down with his bride
in a stone cottage
went back to his smoking jacket
wrote a book and tore it up
they say, I never saw it.

I learned to talk again
in spite of them all
every crowd and Burgomaster
—read by fires, by lakes
ate what I ran across
but killed no people
not for a long time now.

The flesh has not decayed, probably can't.
I carry a cane and that explains the walk.
I dress like a cheap old man
a man with peculiarities
a man you'd leave alone
to live in a shed in the woods.
He'll die, I won't.

He can't live forever
and he doesn't like it when I show up.
I haven't tried that in twenty years.
I accumulate birthdays like everyone else.
He could call. His wife
could call. My only family.
I wonder how it will be without him.

ONE, OR WORDS FOR POETRY

read at Delphi
on the Feast of Saint Nikolaos
at a celebration of Gary Snyder and his work
6 December 1998

air
life

hit the keys

work and word are good words
words for poetry

three, two, one
anything, something, thing

sight is good, the eye,
and good is good, a good word.
Seeing people, watching them climb up the cliff with their kids
kids are good
and people who are alive
in sex and breathing, the body
another good thing as poets never get over saying
which, but which,
for me is the ocean, the sea a better word,
a word to see the sea with,
the sea and its air
and a cigarette with you. A smoke.
All these are words that I could read out loud
for the ones who are gathered to hear.

✦

thank you are good words
typo is too long

as if it matters
as it is matters
it is is an easy typo for if it

Watching you smoke on the side of the bed is good
it would be even better if they could do something about the traffic

✦

any line can be thin
come to terms
to a term

How far from the words do you have to stand?
Wall beyond here, said the hick by the side of the road,
wall up a way there till you come to it.

and the terms we come to terms with are not left
not cut
the terms we come to terms with are not cut
we can use time in a line

a love poem
in love with the word

time is a very good word
in spite of very
short lines are good,
short words
like that line
and the word line

✦

words on a page
food on the tree
and smoke, another good word
favorite of the gods
in spite of another and favorite
what we share with the gods
along with a love of the sea and a weakness for words

and if you were here
that would be better
we could make love
in spite of better, which has too many syllables

the old job of loving
and saying it in words
the old job of being together
and saying nothing

all two in one, after
the one by one

✦

It hides in the short
once said is said
words, core:

if
no end to if
you, I
like the stars
no telling
no counting
tell

light from far in the dark
from old time
points
to which we always want to draw a line
from us to them, as if
the line would start from us
or come from them

but what's a star to do
admire its planets like children who never leave?
or draw a line
through the radio colored clouds

if you think stars think
we have a place for you

✦

now is a typo for know
this is for you and the word you

writing has
too many syllables
poetry is too long
and po-em
and syllable

words like to be mean are good
and to mean is good

problem has two
but sex
and you
and and
have only one.
The End
a short line

made of short words
and in spite of favorite
my favorite line

✦

Laugh is a good word
laughing is too long

by now you can do this by yourself
but yourself is too long
like itself and remember, memory
and words that are even longer
longer being too long
and being. Is is better
but better is too long

love has one, so does count

and this leaves us
without the word without
and without leaving
so we are left
or back
with us.
We can say thank you for is
and and
and words like that
good old that
a good line
all we can do

ONE, OR WORDS FOR POETRY

air is good
see is good
to see is good
to see you
in or out of time
to see you
good words, past death

✦

I forgot blood
another good word
in spite of another
and forgot

✦

we all know
yes and no
and know
and mine
and mind
and I

what do I know
is a good line
how would I know
a typo is good
how would you know

how would you know
if you wrote it before
since before is too long, like memory

15

but you know
is a good line
and you do know
and we can say

the little words
no matter how badly they have been treated
by lazy poets, ads

✦

Anyway
in spite of anyway
life is not too long
and that is not too long to say

even here
with all of you
where we thank words
thank kids
thank those who sail
and thank and
which keeps us going
in spite of going

✦

I don't know but certainly maybe

an awful line
worse if you follow it

wrong way down a one way street
to the mother of all traffic

✦

someone wrote this before and did it better
how would you know
I just hope so, Schreibenleutnant

anyway I forgot to say care
and wine and home
but you want to go home

and go is a good sword
sword is a typo for word
go home

make love is good
make is true

make love true

say honest, sunrise, fire, music, onion
which I forgot along with others that are too long

another end
in spite of another
because in spite of because
and in spite of very
because this loves you very much this says.

✦

smoke is good
we're back to that

smoke good
the fiend said
friend good
fire no good
good, bad
bride of

but we can not say the long name
not his in the first place
of the man who made him

son of
bride of,
the kids
I did not have

say it
bad blood
stopped me
no boy, no girl

life that goes on
as well as it can

in spite of the yelling
in the other room.

✦

right and wrong are fine
and blue
but comma is too long

we have to have blind
form, plant, dog, sand
drown
the blind sea strikes at the hull

at the boat, wet slip on the wood
and the water brings dark to the lungs
fills the breath with jelly
fills the brain with jelly, no room for you
in the only cells you ever had a right to

but enough of death
it takes too long as it is

✦

strong, stark
old words we know
all of them short
like peace, like once
once is a typo for one
like one and I
and I will die
and so will you
as we all know
so what we know
must be said
in short words here

words that mean
in spite of what mean means
does does
and love loves

At least we can say
life lives.
Covers it like a tent.
I forgot rain
Shut up
a good line

✦

I need another
too long but what the hell
I want it in

need it for love

it can't be all the word you
and love makes no sense without another, Bozo

it keeps the cold hot
in the place where
where is here
that can be done
that can be said too
meant and done

✦

love may fail
life will
and if there were we and us and all of that
to know
how fail and bad came
into our language, I should say our words
into the way we are
but what do you care what I say
you are gone from here
anyway if I could say anyway I would say
good bye is cheating but that happens too
everybody breaks the rules.

✦

Are you an angel
or
do you come from God

I would say I am on to something if I could say something

so do you come from God
or not

do you remember my dad
do you remember my mom
do you remember a goddamned thing
or are you just
one of them
the ones
who made the mask up
so that they could lie

    behind the masks
    we know what bastards they are
    thugs pretend to be heroes
    the women are men
    if the tragic poet cried through them to the gods
    it slid right by
    no mask when you talk to a god

If there is another word for angel, say it.
And for another.

✦

The mind can stop
when the words do.
You can find them in here
if you look and if you want
the good words
one of them is you
one of them is air

but not the word I know that you will find
in here with me packed up for you
all in a great big death, a word we don't like
and go on in spite of, thank you very much

bad lines, what can you find in them
yes, here, fine:

✦

Fuck and sun are good words.
Like stretch and think. And but.
But memory is too long.
Tell is a better word
in spite of better
so thank you very much
for the chance to
tell you

in spite of very
and other words like other
that are too long.

Celebrate is too long
but feast is good
and so is wine
and so is bread, which I forgot to mention
along with other things
that are too long to say here
but say and here are good words
so this is good to say here.

ONE TWO

blood in your head
not dust in a box yet
get it down
before the sun takes all of it back to the day
it came from the day

sky in the skull, the sunrise
purple and gray where sky and water meet
your future lurks
eggplant monsters
under the water
rose and butter on top
all cloud and the sun again

money turns to chalk in your pocket
your lover cheats
birds eat your breakfast, your kids
are your parents again
they locked you out and nobody has a key
stars, ice on the path
maybe you'll make it

✦

the space from one to two: fractions
to fall between
into the huge night where dividers slice you
thousandths of you drifting

and the snap from life to death
the way it takes you
last cigarette the one you just put out
there isn't time to open the last book

any fire can be a sacrifice
any day can kill you
any day can bring your lover
any line can be blank

into the glass-flat silence runs a river
molten with mercury, carrying your face

SLIDES

How many days are left before we die?
Today in the city, the only afternoon
we'll ever have, you squeeze my hand like ice.
It's been four years and only now the world,
like the nice waitress, is leaving us alone.
We must have it written all over us.
We have an hour, had. If time remembers,
the afternoon and night we could have chosen
instead are in that hour still. One frame.
Days circle, wait, for some kind of decision.

When rust discovers us, I'll be the one
that never went to you, for all my planning.
The thread broke like a phone bill nobody paid,
the credit card some guy found in my wallet
and used to place so many expensive calls.
All of that time I thought about you waiting,
our feeling, unadvantaged, undiscovered
because not wondered at and taken home.
The mystery was that when I got the bill
the expensive calls had all been made to you.

"Here we are under drawings of trees,
still early in love, with a picnic lunch of wax.
You can see the flowers: they repeat in patterns of six
around the lake. This next one was one noon:
the wind was full of bees, we hid in the plants—
that accounts for our position. The time I wasted
before I met her! life in a slide projector.
This scene is later, after we had grown—
I never will forget who took the picture—
but it isn't true. Come, let me show you others."

Spain has no comment, but Los Angeles
worries me with its mudslides. You are stiff
as breakfast lettuce, and I come to you
like bean soup in Gloucester, hoping one of us
is tired enough from walking around the island
to flip the pictures. Next to those tomatoes
Montreal urges us to buy shampoo
before the revolution, when in movies
the screen wall falls to smudge the audience
flat in their seats and stores close earlier.

I can't keep secrets, not this afternoon
when I finally settled it: this is the day
I let the horse go and moved back to the city.
I call you from the station, then I call you
from the first drugstore. You're at work, then going home
you call this phone booth. From the hotel phone
one block from your apartment I dial your hallway
and we have a good talk. I tell you everything.
Later I call you in bed, and closer than time,
you don't know where I'm calling from, but listen.

Weary as a new animal, I thought
the noise was you. The lampful of scorched flies
stirred as I moved upstairs, my foot asleep,
stuck in remembering the reasons you gave
it wouldn't work out, the story you stopped, that hug
in the windy street (they steered their trucks around us),
letters that burned in shoeboxes and welded
spigots of talk, a bird's nest of projections—
everything slips between this noisy machine
and time as I wait you out, hold, hearing you leave.

We give Proust's Neck to the cat. In fifty years
the National Geographic will discover us.
Till the fourth grade I only learned to print.
"My handwriting's from my mother," I told the angry
old lady teacher, fifth grade, different school,
"she taught me this summer." "Your letters are crude," she said.
Now I teach college. Our house is full of art.
We live here thinking of time and hearing squirrels
drop nuts inside the walls. We fold things under,
wait for the Bomb, and think of having children.

What is there left to do but set these tiles
here in the hall of your building, each like an oyster
carefully clamped to the gray set of this morning?
In sixes they interlock, a system of days
built to a corridor's blind spots. Down the hallway
your separate experience grows like a sugar crystal,
mounting to lunch hour, summoning the elevator.
Partitions have such moments: walls that hang
torn and imperfectly frozen, till clinging flashlights
lie about what can happen and let me see you.

What could we mean to the people in this room?
Even so I am showing them our intimate story
as directly as possible, popcorn on the table.
One picture replaces another as the screen
forgets itself like the future, leaving them free.
They go home to a place where Daniel and Delia
work things out. Or Celia. They live in a world
where poetry readings pause and the poets explain
exactly what they mean: "All elephants
resemble, if you understand, my past."

GEOMETRY OF DAWN

1

In the middle of a mountain I know, she said,
there is a man and a tree of silver.
The leaves of the tree are words.
He shows you a branch, he shakes it,
and deep in the mountain
the words drop like slow fog:
you are beautiful, fated, open,
whatever the leaves say.
You smile stupidly at all this information
until you see that the words have left
spaces on the branch.
These spaces
he proceeds to interpret.

That silver litter, she says,
is the language of men.
God speaks in the sequence of space.
No, I said, the language of men
is binary, the leaf
that is there or not,
itself or not;
the language of God must be every shape at once,
the flow of itself through space.

Very well, she said, I know another story
but this one you must not repeat.
She blew a smoke ring.
I looked for the center
and fell through a torus of cloud
that turned round itself
and would not seem to leave me
all of that night.

2

The rock said, How much of an island
can you recognize?
A wave of rock
on a wave of water, I said.
Not bad, said the rock. Now
what do you mean by wave?
The regularity of space
as it passes through itself, I said.
Good, said the rock, I have a shack
for you and your beloved
to continue to discuss these things
and when you are tired, to sleep,
and when you are ready as water
to flow through each other and shape to yourselves
the image of you together.
You mean speak to the universe, I said,
in its own terms?
That's right, said the rock,
although what could be not our terms
I fail to imagine.

3

I went to the desert and met her on a ledge.
She was playing with her leg and singing
as if to the muscle:

> Many are perfect
> but you are beloved
(she sang, and flexed her foot)
> and so you should dance.

I dreamed of an island, I said,
that was not elemental
so much as it was prime.
There was a wall of ghosts
disguised as a cliff.
It stood between us
and the room of proof.

I was there, she said. I know, I said,
and when you woke up
you faded out of the landscape.
Then I went through the cliff
and found this flower of sound.
Here it is, back from dreams
and for you.

4

There was a boy, she said,
who lived in colors.
He was born in the color of the trunk
of this olive tree
which is also the color of 7 P.M.
in some parts of Massachusetts
and the color of the rock
you spoke with in my dream.

When the boy had tired
of this peculiar gray
he explored the red of this pen
and found himself wherever that color was:
on the ten thousand copies of the cover of that magazine
for instance, or a berry against the snow.
In the end he discovered
a sequence of states of being.

He began with the first, the olive bark,
then moved from the darkest blue
to the purples and yellows, all the way to white.
It is the structure of beginning
after years of trial.
It is child's play, and dawn,
the wall that opens behind you.

So, she said, let's go to bed.
I don't get the connection, I said.
You will, she said.

THE ASTONISHED SPOON

1

Breakfast was short. Karen struck
the red saucer awake
with her busting cup.

She astonished his spoon.
Her strawberries stewed in tea.

2

He gave her
the house and pool.

She ate the pool.

3

Death came to get her
but settled for her car.

She walked toward the ocean
destroying the things in her purse.

4

She lived in the mountains
picking at her head.

In a month she discovered
the skull, that it felt no pain.

Her lips crumbled off.
She found what the jawbone demanded.

5

There was limestone all over the lawn.
The lawyers ticked.
Her husband moved back to the house.

It was a fast thirty-two years
till he heard her
                singing to him at
                breakfast.

They found him
alone on the sunporch:

blasted, holy.

A WELLS FARGO IN SAN FRANCISCO

We walked into a Wells Fargo in San Francisco, and when I asked her if it was all right since my account was in Colorado, a young Vietnamese woman with a great smile directed me to a teller. She was in a stall with short walls and an oak desk, I guess you'd call it a desk, the board you fill out slips on. It was blond oak. The whole place was laid out in careful rectangles with lots of glass, and as it was about one o'clock on a lucky day, the sun was just coming out. I gave the teller my account card and entered my password just as I would at the local bank, and then she asked me how much of my own money did I want. She said it just like that. I was surprised it worked at such a distance.

How did I know the first woman was Vietnamese? The first thing I asked for, before the business about money, was where was a good place to get a cup of coffee, and of course find a restroom, because that was the only way you could get to use one in this neighborhood, which was a little seedy. The fog had made things look cleaner. Lise had suggested asking in the bank, which was why we went in. Getting some money was on second thought. The young woman told us about the café up two diagonal streets, like the side of an X, which was fine with us, in fact we had heard about it, but the woman said that if we wanted Vietnamese coffee, we should go a different way, actually more level, for about two blocks, and then I recognized her, I mean that her face was Vietnamese, not that I knew her. We went uphill to the first café, and each of us read the Sunday comics we found on the table while the other went to the restroom, which wasn't clean but No Problem. No Problem is what they say in Jamaica about practically anything; we've been there. It had been cold until the sun started to come out, and we needed the coffee. She

A WELLS FARGO IN SAN FRANCISCO

had a latte and I had a doppio, which is what they called it on
the painted menu on the wall where you ordered standing before
a high wooden table or board, I don't think you'd call it a desk,
where one man took the orders and made the coffee and the
sandwiches and whatever else they had there and the other man
handled the money. She liked Dilbert the best today. We talked a
long time and kept the table as you can do in a real café, then left
and went to read the brass poems set into the pavement of Jack
Kerouac, which is a block long.

How we came to be in San Francisco is that we had been together
for two years and it was time for us both to see family. So we
went. How I came to meet her was that I failed to for many
years. That was in Colorado. How I came to be in Colorado
was I lived in different places. In one of those places I taught
English at a college for women, and a lot of who I am started
there, falling into today like a spinning maple seed, at least for me
though of course not for Lise, which would take us in a whole
other direction, like going up the family tree of your father or of
your mother. They gave me a desk. The place was called Wells.
It was founded by Henry Wells, of Wells Fargo.

FIVE WEEKS

I look at you more than 24 times a second

This morning I got up
and took the subway to work
or I got up this morning
You were brushing the snow off the car as a surprise
In the barn, the boats under sheets
light hay and nails

Do they like me at work?
The subway is grease, the ads
are like horrible friends
There is no time to work
My headache responds to television

I got up—there was the moon
at six o'clock

I got up again
The moon was there again
It was cold, it was crowded
I went upstairs to wait

I heard you
in the corner

> "Oh write me quickly,
> abandoned in this building.
> Our own time only
> draws together so."

THE CONSTANT LOVER

When you died I stole the priests' secrets and for that
they wrapped me alive in cloth, shut me in stone—
tore paintings and scrolls into strips,
held my neck hard, locked my jaw and broke my teeth
with a belt of words, drove the eyes against their sockets
with the inch from a landscape, shut my forehead flat.
They knotted my arms in repose.
They laid me under a parody of my face
covered with curses.
I wrenched my arm out of its socket, screamed,
beat blind with my back on the stone, felt no stone, died in swaddling!
waited, at the door of your tomb.

In four thousand years they found us and I lived.
When I moved through the camp and killed, you were gone in a crate.
I left my mark on their throats.

Because you are the princess
while you lived I was afraid
for my house, for my life,
for the time I had spent as a priest.
I left my thoughts of your neck, of your arm, for night.
I lay in my house and listened to the wind.
When you died I risked everything
but they laid me near you
in a different eternity.
When I woke, you were gone.

I have my own priests now, burning leaves under my nose.
They think they are in control, with their pendants and mutterings.
In a boat we come to a city.
They push me in a wheelchair, explain
I have facial burns. They help me onto the subway
where people look as they look away, afraid of my power.
They are all of them keeping me from you,
all of them, alone in their anger
which is my anger.

I found you at night on the first floor, *Hall of Kings*,
and strangled the guard while the priest slid away the glass.
When I touched you the wrappings gave way into a vacuum,
collapsed in a pile of cloth. Your body was gone
but away in the night we heard a woman scream.

You live in her now.
I wait on her balcony, strong in the summer air.
The maid tidies up,
some fool of a lover leaves.
With the white growing in her hair
she goes to sleep.
I burst through and take you away.

I have aged you to my age,
there is no other way.
It comes back to your face, the moment of death,
the tissues that dry and tense, that stretch, that wait
for thousands of years in a minute: that revive:
and the eyes are alive
the lips are wet with sleep
every thread in the cloth pulls away from every thread
powders off in a brown wind and the eyes are alive

STAR

1

Time is a wavefront

parallel lines converge

you and I are concentrations within a medium

and the mind is a spider
on the web of space
with the difference that
the web secretes the spider.

2

We turn air into breath
by breathing.

A simple example
of how we get confused.

3

In the mathematics of space
there are certain predictable configurations.
Light pulls to itself,
grows thick into a star.
It spins and makes process

is a locus of process
the way a dimension or two
construct a plane
the way chemicals come together
to break into life.

Take water:
it is just water.
In a random move
it fills itself up with fish.
So now there are fish
and they organize themselves to continue.
They forget they are water
with a way to live.

4

When energy spins around itself
it elements, it forms matter.
Out on the spiderweb
light talks to light:

it is synapse, the jump
from cell to cell
and from the mind to stars.

Light learns how to look,
makes part of itself be an eye.
The neurons fire and know.
I look at you.

So now there is love
and we organize ourselves to continue.

ON THE WAY

for Frank McConnell

The Lord is One.
He can send the Madonna if he wants.

The light that turns the light out
turned it on

But the next time you get a hundred years,
the next time existence lets you into the blood party

This is your body
bloody cracker
This is my body
whose image is nailed to the wall
This is your blood
of bonds, the ones you choose
This is my blood
imagined out of wine

There is a monster on the way to God
and Hell is real. Love takes you there and drops you.

✦

Frank is with the Father, the original J

It never mattered what was on the channel
or how fast we wrote to keep up
when God did the talking

Frank bends at the entry, points
as you enter
on the way to God you happened to take
whoever you happened to be
on the way to God
where the light is and the right words
you were trying to find
and Frank was trying to find
on the way to God, where the ark is
and the right words
for breathing and for what the
actual light dictates:
what Frank meant by shines
and what my father forgot
under the canopy of other pages

      but left a trail that somebody who loved him
      could trace, the principle of light in stars
      the points that point, astronomy of suns
      a shining system cruel as all getout
      pointing back to love as if we could forget it

The notes, the walk
      to Delphi or wherever
or whoever
you were or happened to love
or how you said it
on the way to God,
whoever points it, how the avenues
lay out, in spite of all the other words
or avenues, what gets to be a line
under the canopy of palms or pages,
under the shade my lazy dad preferred,

the way he liked it,
on the way to God
he happened to take
or happened to be
the channel he was
        and always watched till dawn

One line after the other
like the breath with which we thank
as long as the pages hold out,
Frank's breath
No one thought he could take it
they thought he was already done
bowing out of the way like a fiction
        which is why Frank was a critic
for only the right words pass

in spite of the agony that's on the channel
and how we are attuned away from it.
There is a Lord of light, an ark
approached by the right words,
        which is why Frank knelt, no fool,
and pleased the compassionate
on the way to God
the way he happened to take,
ashes in the Chicago River or whatever
        and anyone he loved
on the way to God
he happened to take
and how he said it.

Whoever I happened to be
or loved
or how I said it
on the way to God

we had some of the right words
spelled right and weary for him

along with him and for him
on the way
of counting, which my father took,
of numbers, on the way to ten, 10,
God's favorite.
The way my father took,
        numbers,
and how I took it,
        numbers and words.

Frank made sure he said I love you with his lips,
all he could do

And so we give thanks for the men and women
we loved and found the words for
to tell them and honor them,
standing together
where Frank did it correctly, standing with Celeste
and in a suit, the way it was supposed
to be, ten syllables for every line
in a script that looks like Hebrew,
a ream of pages only they could fill

pointing to the light,
the ark among the correctly lined-up trees,
the whole thing organized the way he likes it.

Our Father
Adonai echod.
We said them both to a box near a hole
on a hill, the ones who cried for Frank and stood
the way he likes it, standing in the light
like friends together, holding hands the way
we tried to say it, and how we tried to love

each other and everyone else, in the right words
on the way to God and standing in the light

The last line, like the breath
        and all the love
he breathed and left behind him,
        on the way
he took again, like a breath, with who he was
and who I am or was and who you are.
Shut up the way he taught me, follow the words
into the silence

alongside on the way
        —if fallen, pick up

        and be kind, see what it needs

the way Frank opened a bottle
        and poured for two,
the light under a glass
with a wink that meant he loved you over the edge
the way God loves you
and says it in the right words,
        over the light
of water, waterfalls
of bugs or language, any way he likes

the way he says it, and my father did,
opening a bottle for the two to drink
in the picnic that he made
        beside the water
opening a bottle of air for you to drink
and say on the exhale whom you loved and who
you happened to be, on the way
to God or

LOVE IF WE CAN STAND IT

—because we do not want it to be easy

or

wherever you were going with the monster you hired

choosing the one you choose forever
    at the last minute
    the way he lost
his last breath, which would be
    as he said over a brandy in the kitchen, like
his last prayer, though he never was pious.
Smoke and the air
    and them you cry for
saying their names before God
so God remembers
the way we do, who love
on the ground, with grass
and water food and words and lose it all

The way he pours a bottle
air and food
    until we say our lesson
in the light and water, everything
he made quiet for you
after love
the way you say it
thanking your lover and everything you saw,
detected, built, and cared about to say
in the right ten terms or one big splotch
because any cornstalk knows how to be
but it matters how you said it, how you loved it
felt and decided, told and were and fucked up
on the way to God, where everyone is sinking
after the wreck, and nobody is coming
if that's the way it goes, at least together
the way you chose and said,
    opening

a bottle of light and air and love and words
the way God does or did and how he said it

together, in the way words have to take it

and love does too—
        tough draw, no matter who
or cards, or words, the way
        he likes to play it,

say all that
before the son of a bitch turns out the lights

especially if you needed them to see
where you were fucking going,
        on the way
to the floor where he left you
        mouthing in the dark
the words your monster taught you
everything you need to say and can't
the thing that finally hit you
or even what you learned from Mr. Right
who uses love and blood and words to teach you
the way he wants it, even if it leaves you
busted on the ground
all that pain looking up
with the end of how you said it
to whom and however
you happened to say it, and
        who gave you life
the way he did and taught it,
the pain that taught you if you wouldn't stop
for anything else, or if you listened only
to love and that was all you heard or said
over the waterfall he poured for you
in the light of words and water
        who gave you all that
bullshit and cruelty to overcome

the teachers he picked
     who gave you a mouth
hunger for life, air in the blood
the way he wants it. Die in the light
that stays on after you go

for the ones you protected
like dust in the corner you wouldn't let anyone sweep
because you loved it or her or him or just
the way you kept or said it

the way he taught you
holding hands together
dying together in the night or dying
in the light on the ground alone
the way he made it
for you to figure, on the way he filled
with trees and light and water,
     friends and muscles,
touch food and breathing, everything you needed
to walk, together, what else did you need?
Even the silence
to fill the way you do.

He lets you talk to him
only in decalogs, two fives, the way
he taught and likes it, music and air and words
the way he likes it, Shining Glory, so
it comes to him in silence, blood and loving,
the way he said it, in the proper language
we had to learn and take the time to read
with old relentless teachers and at night,
our hands together, how he made it, hands
that fit together, tremble hold and write
the way they loved or said it, on the way

✦

ON THE WAY

He finishes everything you love or need
so let him finish this
while we have a drink in spite of everything,
laughing over the glass the way the sun comes up
above the mountains people put between them
waiting for just the right words to come and take them

They wait; we find
the words that take an hour, that take
your blood if they have to, as they take your breath
in the line he gives you, even love and death,
the way he likes it, shutting up
after he gave you air and time to say it,
a tongue to talk with after all that tasting
and light to write with, anything you needed—
the perfect host

And so you lose them, hands out in the dark
for all the ones you listened to or
absolutely needed, like the breath
he gave you with instructions on the box,
a present, like a joke you had to get
before, as said, the Lord of Hosts calls time,
the end, writes down the score, goes home
the long way like Odysseus, island to island,
woman to woman, word to word, the way
he likes and says it, in the tales or not,
making it up before his sleepytime,
the complicated blood and air, until.
And all the pain we muster, all the need
for breathing that we have, the love and how
we say we'll say it, doesn't change his mind.

A mechanic, he accepts that engines fail.
He made the universe of mass and fire
in the first place, blowing out and starting up
whenever, with no grip on little death,
a concept that eludes eternity.
Positive everything is going fine
he tattoos another galaxy on his arm
that curves like space.

No hand is reaching down with help today.
Not for you on the ground, you always knew you'd crash
alone and hate yourself for being stupid.

So we say we don't care, we're too busy for you and your demands—
what Eden means—but what we mean is, if
you have any decency turn out the light
and leave us to do what we have to
with that one more breath you bet we'd never take.
Whether you're God or a local demon
this is a place
we don't care that you made or anything
you might have wanted, this is us,
Celeste and Frank, or
        the writer and the dying everyone
who drinks or eats or says it, breathes, enjoys
the picnic, waterfall
        rocks over the water

And that's how words and demons, love and farmland
teach us to use the mouth, for kissing, biting
or talking or sucking, and the eyes to cry
water, which they can do while they are seeing,
the way our hero likes it
but while he dwells in his Oneness
we came up with sex.

Even incarnate, he remained alone.
He's One and had his first fight with a couple.

A math with just one number gives the same
answer, no matter what division works
a thing into itself or square root squares.
It is good to know that answer; he always does.
He stands at the absolute center of knowing it.

We have our two, three, and the wild card, zero:
nothing or ten, like character—at best
the absence that makes huge the hole it leaves
and everything before it.

The way we remember, record—the way we count—
catches the details like an auditor
which is why my father was an accountant.

He leaves us on the ground, a bed, to say
what he wants to hear
but we say what we say.

Respect us in our death, Lord hear our prayer
and get out, do something in Eden, it's empty.
You can stop the blood
when we're through with it.

If you have to, you can fill out the reports
to yourself in the words we taught you, like a dean,
because the tale ends here, or all we're telling.
You turned the lights out and you can't complain
what we do with the darkness, with the lack of breath
to tell each other, not you, in our language.

Count to ten over and over, count it in tens
until they count to your aspects and your fingers.
We'll figure out a way, we always do
in spite of you
and all the life you take away like sheets.
The corpses tell you nothing, buried or burned,
and that's the way we like it. Count to pi,
Lord hear our prayer. All the time we had
or thought we had is turning into space—
the universe, and then a couple of feet.

We couldn't give a damn about the bills
so turn the juice off, put another name
on the door of the office, change the bed, with all
the blood and snot we made and you erased,
bleaching us out of the world, and all our woe.

It's over our own bodies that we say
all that we loved and did in spite of you
and all the death that lets you just go home.

✦

A story please, to think about instead.

Once upon a time
the frog was king, and the princess
knew it, and the frog pond dried
like tears when the rain stops. God can't tell the difference
between a rain of frogs and blood and water
but the frog explained it patiently and then
turned out the light and made it with the princess
and had a smoke, which with his froggy lips
was a trick so Irish he became a prince,
bought drinks for the house and slept: This is my heart,
he said, and you can have my body too
but only when the princess falls asleep.

THE FIRST ONE IS PAPER

On the anniversary
of our marriage
I watched
the sun set
in a lake
of trees.

I said
"I divorce you"
as the sun
clustered over
in black
and the branches
closed.

It was a silhouette,
a fist,
a calm.
It was a ceremony.

SESTINA: LUNCH

Joan takes the cherry soda out for Willy,
heats up the coffee for herself and Mike,
makes a big tuna salad, yells at Sara
to set the table instead of scaring Pat
with her rubber knife, trips over Judy's
jumprope, rights herself, and thinks of Fred.

"It's lunch!" she hollers, wondering whether Fred
remembers her or cares. In rushes Willy,
red from building a snowman; in comes Judy,
red from smashing it. Next thing she knows, Mike
kisses the back of her neck. A shriek from Pat
at just that moment lets them know that Sara

has her hands free; the table's set, then. Sara
wobbles the knife in Pat's face: killer. ("Fred
wanted kids, I didn't," Joan thinks.) Pat
gets strong all at once and hits her sister. Willy
runs back outside to finish Frosty. Mike
takes the knife and scolds the girls. Then Judy

cries, "Mommy, help me!" Willy bashes Judy
with snowy fists. Joan clenches up and Sara
relaxes, turning to smile at Mike.
Joan knots. Between Mike and Fred
there isn't much difference, and just now even Willy
reminds her of the men. She looks at Pat,

all blunder and fist, and her head hurts. Pat
goes to her seat. Across the table Judy
settles and smirks as Daddy wallops Willy
for the second time this week. Abruptly Sara
serves herself tuna Just Like Mommy. ("Fred
wanted kids, I didn't. So I took Mike.

I wanted to be free, I wanted Mike.
He said just one, and now look.") Pat
piles on the jelly, eating hate. ("Where's Fred—
the Army someplace? Look at Judy.
He'd laugh at me like that. And look at Sara,
ready to kill someone.") Joan turns to Willy

and pours him soda. Willy likes her. Mike
puts his hand on her leg. Sara smiles at Pat,
makes plans for Judy. All of them look like Fred.

THE TREES

I will not praise God but I will praise the trees.
I will praise the strong grass and the catalog of ferns
and the names in each language for water.

I WAS WEEPING FOR BEAUTIFUL JAPAN

1

The cherry
heavy with rain

the air, water-beaded
bent with the weight of it

only the bridge creaks
only the cicada

night of full blossom
white in the giant moon.

2

Just before all the
lights went on, I

told you I loved you,
heard your heart breathe. We

lay down and opened ourselves
to a year of peace

when a china rose opened up the sky
and the whole place scattered like feathers.

3

I was weeping for beautiful Japan,
the valley and cherry
and what was around these bones.

It is a wet evening, and you and I
have gone a long way together.
Listen under this gate to my story:

> There was a woman who would have lived a thousand years
> for she knew all the names of quiet and had the dark eyes of
>   the blessed.
> One day the sun came to earth and took her away.
> She shines like the fury of a hundred deaths in an instant

in the star that chills
the dead center
of our being here.

4

I have been here
with your hair against my hand
as your head moves, kisses

and if it had not been
and the garden not been

the night left alone
in its burning

there would still be the breath of your dreams
on my sleep, on my peace.

TWO GREEK WOMEN

1

Athanasía loved Christina's big hips,
the birthmark down the left of her body,
her thin lips and happy laugh.
Christina sometimes could not take her eyes
away from Athanasía's, black as her hair.

Christina's lover was a knockout
and not just because she's someone you're reading about,
either made up or impossible to meet.
The lines of her face and body ran into each other,
ran your eyes in oval swoops.
It took adrenaline to look at her
and roused it in your core when you got it that
you'd finally met the woman you were sure
didn't exist. She could toss fire.
There was saffron in her hair when she came close.
In a filmy dress that brushed her ankles she
could leave Christina out of breath
like it hurt to breathe
like for two minutes she'd have to sit on a bench.
They both had olive skin.

They went on a trip.
Athanasía wanted to go to the mountains,
Christina missed the sea.

They quarreled, made up, made coffee,
looked at a map and found the mountain island.

Built from her birth to be faithful to one man
and give her perfect figure to ten children,
Athanasía met her lover at the beach.
Christina was looking at shells,
crouched a foot into the water
where the surf made a little bidet
and picking them up unless spidery legs grappled out
but held the others to the sun that turned her skin
red in shadow while the shell gleamed like a cloud.
Athanasía buckled, ripe and helpless.
It took a half an hour to find the guts
to crouch beside her, reach for a blue shell.

If they were a lemon, Christina was the rind
and Athanasía the wet mesh of channels, food for the seeds
if the lemon hadn't fallen into a market
and onto a table, sliced for two Greek women.
Each thought the other was the juicy part,
the sting that wakes the tongue; each thought herself
the strength the other built, the rind
protecting the yellow meat,
stretched to hug it all around,
felt strong and pliant
from giving love and having her to love.

Athanasía loved the beach—needed mountains.
It was a difference of air, between two kinds of air
for Athanasía, and not the sand against
the floor of pine needles, not the ocean smell
against the sap. Air filled her differently;
the rest of us, we just breathe.
Her being rocked—each breath a memory
of a trip the sky took through her.
Christina lost her vision in the sea,

felt in her body the blind roll of the water.
If some of their tastes were different as water and rock
still both of them liked
to cook, read, watch for comets;
both of them noticed everything,
both felt the need
to tell the truth and make up stories, not lie.

Only tales are worth telling. Everything else you can say.
Love should last longer than it takes to tell
the lovers' story. Such love is a condition,
as there as a place. It has two women in it.

Stories and marriages begin with hope
for right going to right ending.
When things go wrong
we don't say all our time was nothing
and forget it. We would not do it again
with that bitch, that bastard, but we would do it again.
We take the dive, then, into love and them.

✦

My heart is wet with beating.

Drink my mouth, she said.
I would but the first time I saw you I went blind.
Let me help you find me
she said in the pulsing dark.

    Eventually
    tell the wrath of Christina
    lightning washed of love
    striking, striking
    the face, the idea

and the rage as bad as death of Athanasía—
her hair would knife you,
red bolts in her knuckles!

Her pet name, Asia: ancient, a woman of parts.
It was ah *see* ah in the longer name
but *ay* zhah. English. It kept the guards confused.
Christina called her that in bed
when they were tired, going off to sleep
and in the kitchen too or on the street—
Athanasía in moments of awe and anger.
When she had to, Christina chose each word, resenting
the spelling out. In the same moods Asia went silent.
They could drive each other crazy or let it go.
It depended how angry they were or how afraid
of losing the other by saying something wrong
or how dumbstruck by the fact of the beloved,
as a pilgrim who has walked three hundred miles
planning a speech goes silent at the door.

Vacations and odysseys for them, not tours.
They went to the mountain island—packed their hero boots,
wore sandals. The highway ran
into an open ending or a closed one
—down to the harbor, not telling.

2

With her long legs she gripped the tree,
climbed for the fruit. Ramón saw his sky woman
and lost his mind with longing, for a minute he was really crazy.

Chris rounded the path, saw Asia and held up a hand
to catch the fruit she threw, laughed as she caught it.

Two Greek Women

I found a cave, Chris said, you've got to see it.
At the bottom of the tree Ramón tried to help Asia down

and she took his hand politely
and she firmly let it go.

He picked up his junk and went back
to the worst existence possible in paradise.
It should not have been a torture
to lack, and only one thing.

✦

A story Christina told only when she knew Asia well:

Chris touched her finger into her mother's ashes
and put them to her lip, last kiss.
Then she took a pinch and ate it,
to take her mother's strength and love inside her
to go with her always.
She took another bit and ate it crying,
ate more and couldn't stop.
She left the big black rocky parts alone
and knew at the end she'd eaten a lot of coffin
along with the eyes that were ashes, the cheeks that were ashes,
the skin of the fingers that had stroked her forehead
when she was little and had a fever, so cool.

✦

They ate fruit and trotted down the path and dropped
their packs on the sand. The beach looked up to the mountain
up to the sky.
When they lay down in sunglasses, Chris took Asia's hand
and called her Asia. Asia said nothing.
When the sun moved over the sky
and they were alone on the cooling beach
they went all the way, then swam out to the first stars.

✦

LOVE IF WE CAN STAND IT

To write about women, two women, if invited:

It's the outsider's privilege to come in from outside
still knowing how it looks, how the lights of the house
glare yellow a kilometer away.
If we are excluded from Chris and Asia's love
because we want one of them to love us instead,
we're out of luck and it is not their problem.
They think they have problems, the freezing traveler says,
maybe pebbles on the carpet or in their shoes.
We go back well fed to the isolating storm,
tightening our coats against the awful wind
of emotional wreck that hurtles through our ears
and down to the skin outside the bladder,
freezing the skin of the crotch. Our hosts were kind.

✦

When three stars come out, the Jewish day begins.
Christina was not a Jew but had from childhood
counted her days the same way, evening to evening
because night was the best time
and the stars were the best part of it.

Everybody loved the moon. It was boring
how many people wrote and sang about it.
For her it became a reminder of how love
was understood by idiots, taken in vain.
She respected love as deeply as a teenager
all of her life. It was the ancient text
on which the other texts were built, the glow
in the brightening iris sharpened with desire.
Its only ties with the moon were bloody:
periods. Its danger was being known
and not being able to live without
a person who could do anything.
Anything can be gay, of course, and full—

no end to the surprises Asia could draw
from the flowerpot of ideas on her head,
no end to the deep pull of her gentle rolling
into position for loving in the morning.

✦

Works and days:

The trouble with getting good at anything
is you have to do more of it. Finally they want you.
Both of them had careers, could work for hours,
made space for days and weeks to be together
and take vacations, built their days to bed
where ice was spread before them in the desert
and each of them was a pitcher, each a glass.

✦

You walk into a bar. Athanasía says Let me introduce you,
takes your arm and you thank her because you don't know anyone
or the language, and a man from the village says
Do you have A girlfriend or A boyfriend?
You say no, and he picks up his drink and says
You should consider our Athanasía
and you look at her and she is looking at you
and you forget your mind and kiss her.
Her lips shake a little and open an eighth of an inch
and you say Consider her? I would die for her
and she says just to you while everybody laughs
You won't have to, and you sit down together
and she says This is a game.

✦

Our polysyllabic lovers sometimes strayed.
It was awful: all that failure, all that coffee,
and the visions that wouldn't stop, the kind you have
when everything around you falls apart
at once and you see the disaster of your life
without her. It happened in the second month
to both of them, the desire to fool around
and find out whether or not they wanted to
come back. Christina was first. They told each other.
They weren't from another planet—all this hurt
and almost ruined them, as it has brought others
down, and their houses with them, kids and lawn.
Completely blown away, the sense of faith
rots like a fruit you wouldn't want to pick
but won't fall off the branch. Just the wrong
pressure at the wrong time can flatten it
and make any trust or further congress between you
out of the question, like sleeping on a beehive
or jumping into the pot. Grief leaves and doesn't.
What dies in you, you have to do without.
If rage can fuse the ashes into bricks
it can make a cellar and a fireplace.

You feel trust when it's gone, something picked off
like a melon from your vine; it leaves a silence
as when the dinner guest leaves after breakfast
and you realize you want more talk but don't,
want to have more love for people but you don't.
You have this house, this mate, this life, and these
mistakes with the medals on the mantelpiece
of your eminent domain as an eminent adult
or anyway in your sack if you're on the street
and in your head if you have nothing else
and if you're an idiot with brains on top of your head,
not even there but in the imagined world
around you, which if seen can begin to look good
to the ones whose job is never to forget a thing,

to be there when they said, to get it done,
to do it all, to do it all on time,
by close of business, by the time she's home.
You made your world. Maybe you broke it.
Maybe you can fix it, slowly as a bone mends.
Breaking the chains of fidelity they saw
more chains around them and went after those
with hacksaw and crowbar till the cell was full
of black fallen metal. Then they kissed and took
the voluntary bond of true chaste lovers,
to fuck each other only and be kind.

✦

Christina hated frogs, and so
there were no frogs in the house.
Asia counted the steps in every staircase,
the seconds of water when she filled the kettle,
the strokes when she brushed her teeth—
a count she forgot whenever the thing was done,
the stairs descended, out on the sunny plaza.
If Asia found a bug, she'd take it out.
Christina would stomp or swat and clean it up;
flies drove her nuts, mosquitoes were a
mistake, and fleas, she hated fleas so much
she wouldn't have a dog, and she loved dogs.
She liked butterflies and did try to help them out
through a door or a window, careful not to touch
the wings or they die her oldest aunt had told her.
She was drawn to the ocean, the beach, but with a difference.
Christina always thought that she would drown
and not as a suicide: it was terror
not to breathe, to breathe water.
It was her fate; she dreamed it
a couple of times; it scared her on a boat trip.
She never told anyone but Athanasía.

✦

Christina gathered sea shells while her lover
brushed the sand out of her long hair after a swim.
Christina cut hers short five years ago
to define herself as much as not to hassle
with hair all the time. It was red, the dark flat red
of a Greek. For her lover to have
the long black hair and the hassle was her luck.
She loved the smell of it, rubbed her cheek in it.

The sun set, and they walked a half an hour
to the place they were staying, where they had a drink
at the bar by the pool and bought more cigarettes.
Athanasía had acquired the habit
at twelve, when everything was a flash
and she was the flashiest thing in it.
Christina wouldn't let anything control her
so she bought a pack a week, one more for deadlines,
and bummed a few but hardly made a dent
in the pack a day that Asia put away.

Athanasía had a line of hair
Christina loved to tongue, down from the navel
and black and fair at once, so soft it curved.
Bed is the best place if you use it right

    Come
    I'm listening for you

and they used it. Showered off the sweat and grease
and sand bits, washed their hair, flipped on the tube,
went out when they were dressed and had the special.

✦

Athanasía went up the wonderful mountain
before Christina woke. She lit a rock
and threw the fire back and forth, then sat

Two Greek Women

with her back against a big wide tree and laughed
a laugh that split the clouds; the sun came down
and made a tent around her, opened her skin
to the endless air. It was then the sky swooped down
and through her lungs and heart, up her neck like a song:

> Athanasía means immortality.
> Everybody wants me but
> nobody can have me.

A purple flower curled to meet the sun.
The smell of the forest went strong, and even shade
took on the smell of something deep and old
waiting in a corner, under every leaf,
each darkness a piece of the quilt on which is patched
our fate, but in a code of strips and colors
we need the sun and codebooks from the gods
to read. It's lucky that our eyes learn shadow.
Athanasía read among the leaves
messages in her second mother tongue.

Christina rustled up breakfast: coffee,
yogurt and honey, strawberries and bread
from the market so they wouldn't have to depend
on the restaurants. Hardly eight; she took
her coffee to the balcony, read her book,
finished the pot and figured out the plot
but read to the end in spite of that.
She did her exercises, made more coffee.
Athanasía came back radiant
with her hair a mess, her shirt torn at the shoulder
when she'd run through clustered trees. Down went her pack,
out came the rocks she gathered on the trail:
one purple with facety cracks, one sandy rose.
For the two of us, she said, a present for you.
They go together, I could get a bag.
I've got one, Christina said. The jewels of the road,

rocks translucent like crystal, went in a leather pouch
tied close with a thong. She never lost the stones.
Out came the yogurt, honey, bread, and fruit,
and down they went smack on their chairs and ate their fill
and smoked and had more coffee and started to talk.

Human evil has no limit, Christina said
in English. She was strict: Greek has no word
for evil. Greeks use *kakos* bad, *lathos*
mistake, like As a person he's a mistake,
but the words back off before the will to wrong,
seething dark power, that Christina meant.
And she smiled. That stopped Athanasía from
trying to talk her out of it at once.
Christina in the Bible could be a judge
like Deborah but never a prophet; when she tied
herself in knots and swept away the world
she was weak, and Athanasía always thought
the weak were dangerous. Chris went on in Greek:

I've learned to watch out, maybe too much but
I'm here, they're not, I have a perfect life
with you and that's all I care about. I just
notice things like you'd notice the smells in a toilet.
Politics is dead; thinking you can make a difference
is dead, a fool's idea. All people want
is a house on an island with olives that pick themselves.
And a straight world to come back to. And TV.
Do you know how they hate us? If the Colonels were back,
they'd outlaw homosexuals first thing
and all the Christian Orthodox would cheer.
They can use our identity cards to find the Jews
already, with everyone's religion stamped on them
already; can you imagine what would happen
if the idiots in this country got together
with the dopes and the morons, nobody could stop them.

Athanasía said, Your problem is idiots? Again?
and Christina said Yes. You had a bad morning?,
Athanasía asked, and Chris said No,
I had a lovely time and so did you.
But I can't stop thinking how they ruin things.
I tolerate how stupid people are
but the stupid things they do, no. Everyone
just shoves, they shove you out of the fucking way
if you're different, and if they can they put
your ass in jail. I never told you but
they fired Nick. Athanasía whirled with a
What? and Christina lit a cigarette.
The day before we left, she said, and absolutely
nobody said it was because he's gay.
They would not even give him a letter of reference.
Why didn't you tell me, Asia said
and Christina answered, It was too much crap.

Athanasía leapt to the conclusion.
You're afraid of losing me, she said; Christina
put down her cup and stopped like an express.
You see people acting badly and you think
I'm just like them and you can't trust me either.
You should think more of me. Or don't you know
the difference? Would just anybody do?
Maybe it's not the other ones, it's me—
you think I'm the shit and you're yelling at everyone else.
Do you want me to leave, is that it, or
is the problem that I went up to the mountain
without you? Fine. From now on, only beach.
Where'd my suit go? Are you scared to love a witch?
Stop it, Christina said, I'm sorry, please.
You're right, you're right and I'm the idiot.
I didn't mean to hurt you and of course
I know you're not the same as everyone else.
I'm sorry I didn't tell you about Nick
and I'm sorry I brought the whole thing up this morning.

Athanasía said Don't worry, but
Athanasía worried just the same.

✦

Athanasía felt around and found
a poet on the dark side of the island.
She felt the call inside her, like a pull.
Heavy with nuts, the trees were heavy with nuts
around her, there were birds, there was a grotto,
the walls were pressed fire, the water was full of squid
impossibly bright, all colors, a green one slid
around a blue, its arms like floating moss,
cups folding water, and there was no way
to find her if she didn't dream you in.
She lived on nuts and fish, she burned a lamb
to the gods on Friday, sent a book a year
to her publisher in Athens by means unknown.
Athanasía grabbed Christina's hand
when the vision hit her, said We have to rent
a boat, now, we have to do it now.

Halfway around the island Christina saw
a cloud outside a cave; the sky stopped being
blue; in the dusk Athanasía steered.
Then they were facing the immensely present
woman of wisdom, master of the tongue.
She handed them, of course, a bowl of blood
and they had to drink it. Athanasía took
hers down in a rush; Christina almost fainted
but drank the horrible syrup swallow by swallow.
The poet drank the last and brushed the tadpole
clots from her lips with her big hand, made them sit.

She told Athanasía, You are a witch.
You take your power from the air and earth,
from spirit plants and stones; you are a flower
clutching an angry bee that rips your walls.
As water finds the beach, you find your home.
She told Christina, You are a warrior.
You try to make your enemy come true.
Honey and murder are your drink, but love
suns the desert where you go to ease your thirst.
That birthmark shows how hard you fought to live;
I like it. Children, both of you, to fix
the world with kindness, lust, and talk. Beware
the unexamined and examined love.
In the meantime try these nuts. They cracked the shells
and laughed together, suddenly at ease.
Then they were back at sea. Then turning in
the boat, getting their deposit back, and sinking.

They fell to the sand and held their heads.
We must be careful, Athanasía said.
I love you, said Christina.
Your power is all these colors. Asia—Hush,
said Athanasía, be quiet, I know.

◆

To make the world a fit place for our love,
Christina toasted. *Vlita*—boiled weeds
milder than spinach—fried fish, cheese, retsina
were spread before them in the purple sunset
of the outdoor restaurant that faced the sea.
Peace, clinked Athanasía, in our place.
Can you live with a warrior, Christina asked.
Don't joke about it, said Athanasía;
sometimes I think you could tear everything
down with your irony—you never rest.
Now wait, Christina said, you mean I can't

talk openly with you whatever I'm thinking?
Don't say you want me putting on a mask
to make you happy, putting on a show.
Of course not, said Athanasía as
she took Christina's hand, I want you real
and open with me, otherwise there is
no point. The differences are there; we can't
ignore them or talk about them, I don't know,
but masks are wrong. Bad jokes are wrong.
So, bravely said Christina, what's the problem?

The problem is the differences themselves,
Athanasía answered. I may be
the wrong one, not the woman that you need.
Don't say that, said Christina. It's not true.
OK, Athanasía said, I won't.
I'll talk about the unexamined love
I think is perfect, something you can feel
is always solid, never questioned, though
the word makes one sound stupid to prefer it.
The examined love, you do that, and you sound
like a doctor or a policeman getting facts.
I'm saying that you can't break off an ear
from a statue to make sure it's marble, not
if you want the statue. Some things you must learn
to leave alone, and one of them is me.
Not all the time, I don't mean that, don't freak.
I just think you'd be happier if you took
it easy; it would be more fun for you.
So much surrounds us that is only beauty,
perfect as oranges from Epidavros,
rich as the wine in your mouth when we drink and kiss.
Oh Christina, how I wish that you could trust me
as much as you say you do, just fall into
my arms and let everything go, forget to know.
It isn't what you think as long as you

can stop your thinking when it's right to stop.
Sometimes it doesn't matter what you say,
it's that you're saying it. By now you hate me.

Leaning across cold food Christina said:
I love you, I don't hate you. It's because
I want you so much sometimes I get scared
of losing you. That's all it is. I know
it's irritating and awful and I'll stop,
I promise. But you know I never trusted
anyone in the way that I trust you.
You know me inside out, I tell you every
bit of my life—OK, I know, too much.
I talk when I get nervous, I use words
like other people use their hands or get
tics. It's OK, Athanasía said.
It's just, Christina said, sometimes I think
you judge me from the safety of your silence.
When I talk to you, I think sometimes you don't
want to take a risk; it takes a risk to talk.
How can I know I'm reading every silence
right? Do you know I work to figure you out
every day? The only time I'm sure
I'm right is in our bed, and then I know
what everything means, I know you like my skin.
Athanasía answered, I'm a bitch.
You shouldn't have to say all this to me.
I shouldn't make you. You go on and love
the way you want to, say whatever you want.
What happened, said Christina, did an angel
bash you over the head? No no, her lover
answered, I didn't want another fight
and I saw where I was wrong and where I hurt you.
Now, are we going to order again or leave?
I want the fish hot, I want the *vlita* steaming

and the sharp cold wine against it. Said Christina,
Maybe we should go out, and Asia laughed.

And after that they packed and headed back.

3

Bread, cheese, and coffee sent them on their way:
Athanasía to the traffic, cursing
the one-way streets that changed last month, Christina
on a train to the stinking din of central Athens.
Athanasía made her visions real
at a drafting table; she'd designed a boat
that wasn't hovercraft but cut the water
faster than ferries, graceful as a sail.
She'd gotten two promotions out of it
and now was working on a kind of pier
that filtered out pollution as the water
ran under it and didn't kill the fish.
Christina wrote computer programs that
were famous for their brevity.
She'd studied astronomy until they said
that stars were points on the celestial sphere,
not burning suns in space. She didn't want
to solve a position, she had a telescope.
Studying logic led her to computers.
Abstraction set in order suited her
especially when it did not pretend
to be or to erase a thing she loved.
She ruled the computer because she did not care.
So both of them were designers, both were set
on working well and making lots of money.
They loved each other and they shared a flat.
What they didn't have in common, they could manage.
Their life was just like toast out of the oven,
ready to melt the butter; everything swam

in every color round no obstacle
like the tropical fish Athanasía bought.

✦

It came upon her suddenly, like flu:
she had to get away from Christina.
Whatever Asia said, Chris would only change,
and that would do nothing about the heart of it.
There's nothing wrong with you,
she wrote in a note, it's me, I've got to be
alone. I really hope it's not forever.
She took her stuff and left—more than you'd take
for a weekend trip but less than moving out.
Christina read the note and went berserk.
You horrible fucking bitch, I never loved you,
never, she screamed through her teeth, why don't you burn
in hell, why don't you die—
but Christina couldn't say that one and cried.

After two days she threw Athanasía's
plants out, dumped the fish, and took the pictures
down that her face was on, and went to work.
Athanasía came three hours later
when she was sure Christina would be gone.
She stood there like a frozen waterfall.
A careful, lovely thing broke in her mind.
She leaned against a bookcase, nauseated
with power, and her love dropped like a roof
in an earthquake. Every vestige of Christina
she saw around her had to be destroyed.
She did not do all that, but she took down
the other pictures, ripped the bottom sheet,
decided to clear out her half of the kitchen,
and left the love note she had brought in ashes.

✦

They met in a taverna, by design.
It was Athanasía who had called.
She was staying with her mother till she found
a flat near work; her life was all in boxes,
her heart a mess, her anger and her loss
confused.
            She'd had a dream in which they met
like Japanese monsters in the skies of Athens,
hurtling bolts of flame and roaring thunder.
Christina had winged sandals and a shield
and meant to kill; one weapon after another
materialized in her hand, and what she threw
came hard, drove true, and emptied the air around
its passing. Wounds her weapons left were gory
and full of feeling, hurt you in your heart
while the wound bled and flesh curled away from it, showing bone.
Athanasía was hit in the breast and thigh
on the right, and her left shoulder was all blood.
Her right arm worked. She gave it energy
from all the land below; the power went out
across the region, there were earthquakes,
seas swelled with waves and whitecaps,
all boats were canceled, tourists checked their watches
while time stopped in Athanasía's hand
and she threw the death of spirit at her lover.

Christina was knocked over and sucked empty.
She fell into the harbor at Piraeus
and rocked the giant boats; five kiosks washed
into the station, cars dipped over, birds
screamed, and pedestrians caught up in the flood
surfed or went under, grabbing balconies.
Christina pushed off from the mucky bottom
and roared up, curving easily as a diver
drops from the top board; into sky she rose
and drew her enemy back into battle.

She knew what evil was: Athanasía
with her gutless lack, the failure of her faith
in the love they had, the vacuum where she should
have glowed with trust, and all the lying she did,
saying she loved and saying she would stay
and covering up her feelings, even when
they talked in bed—a black hole sucking light.
Into the absence that had been her lover
she hurled a hungry net of sky-blue fire,
then threw a dagger where she felt the breast
should be and found it; Athanasía fell
into the air, her heart exploded mush.

I don't know what it was, something you said,
began Athanasía when they'd ordered.
Christina was no fool and on her guard
as if against a snake against this flaky
rejecting stupid woman who didn't love her.
She volunteered: My thoughts on human evil,
which of course has nothing at all to do with us,
pure spirits of love that we are. To perfect women,
she toasted, and they wryly drank. They ate
the calamari while it still was hot
and Athanasía said, That wasn't it.
It was the joke you made about the prophecy.
That wasn't a joke, Christina said; I meant
we have to find a way to talk about
what she said about us, like that I was a warrior.
Athanasía said, I thought that you
were making fun of her, and I am never
wrong about things like that but this time I
was wrong and I apologize. All right?
Thank you, Christina said as formally
as if she held a cup of English china

instead of ouzo and the crumbly bits
of fry left on the plates, the squeezed-out lemons.

We're like those lemons, Athanasía said.
We used to be full when we were with each other
like we belonged together as one lemon
and now we're separated we are empty
of all our juice and flavor, all used up.
There was nothing that you did. It was that I
decided there was something wrong with you
and screwed your world up. Elegantly put,
Christina said, and now she was a Greek
making plans across the table, deciding whom
to fleece and whom to trust, at least today.
But I was hard to be with, Chris continued;
something got to me I couldn't leave alone.
Even today I don't know what it was.
I'm not angry. I just don't want to get ruined.
You reached inside of me because I let you,
only because I let you, and you pulled
my heart out like a glob that's blocked the drain.
I can't stop feeling that; it's not a grudge,
there's nothing past about it. Let me heal it,
Athanasía said. I don't deserve it
and I can't ask but I'm asking. Please, Christina,
I'm opening myself to you completely
and whatever you say will go in all the way
so the next thing, be careful, OK? just what the next
thing is you say, and when you're done please take me
home to your bed, so that's where I wake up.

Christina stopped herself before she said
anything of the cruelty she felt
or the welcoming kindness, hope of finding joy.
I wanted us together, she began.
Whatever, I should not have killed the fish

and I'm sorry about that. You have left a lack
no one but you can fill—that's if you can.
But I'm safer without you and to some extent
I do not recognize you. If I want you
it has to be new, from the present where I live,
not from the past, that sunny past with trips.
That's busted like plates in an argument, it's gone.
That's right, start over, Athanasía said
and shut her mouth. There was a perfect silence
in which the waiter brought the lamb and salads.

I'm tired of being angry at you, Christina
said, putting down her fork. I'm tired
of hating you, but I don't dare to love you.
You could leave me again, you could even wake up
straight some morning and say you have to have
this guy you met at work, you could decide
my thinking isn't right for you again.
You take that risk, Athanasía said.
I take it every day when I'm with you.
You question everything when things are fine,
you wonder if I love you when I love you.
You take the heart out to be sure it's working.
Stop thinking all our happiness away
so we can live in peace and be true and strong
with each other the way I want, the way you want.
Your heart is true, Christina said, and I
would love to trust it. I would love to feel
that this time it is really me you want.
Athanasía kissed her. So, Christina said.

And so they ate and drank together as friends
begin to know each other after years
they both have been away on voyages,
noticing every change in the old companion
and facing each other across a richly laden

table, their weapons sheathed, their glasses full,
but circling each other in their minds like cats.

✦

They found a new apartment near Asia's job.
It had a studio with lots of light,
a full-sized kitchen, and a bedroom with
a balcony. They lived together there
and healed the place that has two women in it
talking, two Greek women talking about love
and being it, the source for two Greek women
to draw from as together they became
a pattern for the bravery of love
love if we can stand it
and for the best we make of what we are,
the gift of being we honor in sacrifice
to the gods who guard and bless the places where
we live, where our love beats, where the winds toss boats
and we almost drown, all losing everything,
but somehow tumble to the beach and home.

Lightning Source UK Ltd.
Milton Keynes UK
UKOW041840271112

202871UK00001B/8/P

9 780857 289216